How to Draw
Dinosaurs

Barbara Soloff Levy

Dover Publications, Inc.
Mineola, New York

Bibliographical Note

How to Draw Dinosaurs is a new work, first published by
Dover Publications, Inc., in 1995.

International Standard Book Number

ISBN-13: 978-0-486-47908-8
ISBN-10: 0-486-47908-0

Manufactured in the United States by RR Donnelley
47908005   2016
www.doverpublications.com

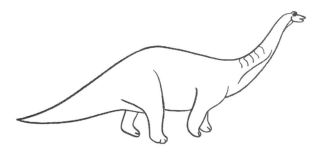

Appearances to the contrary, the Age of the Dinosaurs is not yet over. Today, these mighty lizards are more popular than ever. Now you can create your own, along with lots of other prehistoric animals.

To draw them, just follow the step-by-step diagrams on the following pages. Some erasing is called for, so be sure to use a pencil, not a pen. To get started, let's draw the Albertosaurus on page 2. First draw a large oval for the body and a smaller one for the head; connect the two with curved lines forming the neck. Erase the part of the body joining the neck (and a bit of the head where it joins the neck). Add the legs, tail and mouth; then add details like features and spots. Erase all unwanted parts of lines. It's just that simple!

How to Draw
Dinosaurs

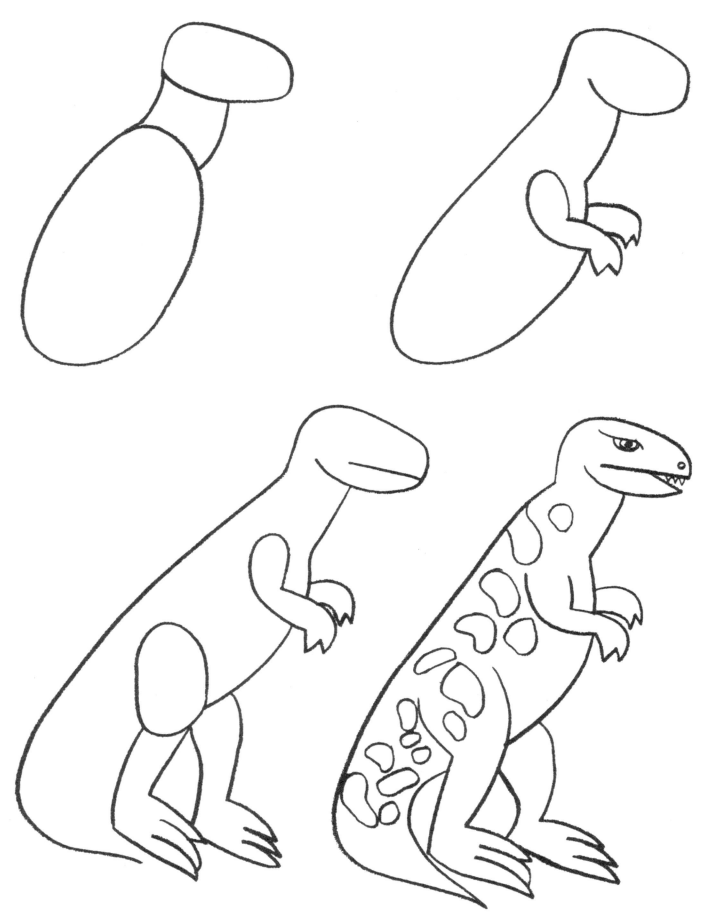

2   Albertosaurus

4   Ankylosaurus

6   Apatosaurus

Practice Page

Practice Page

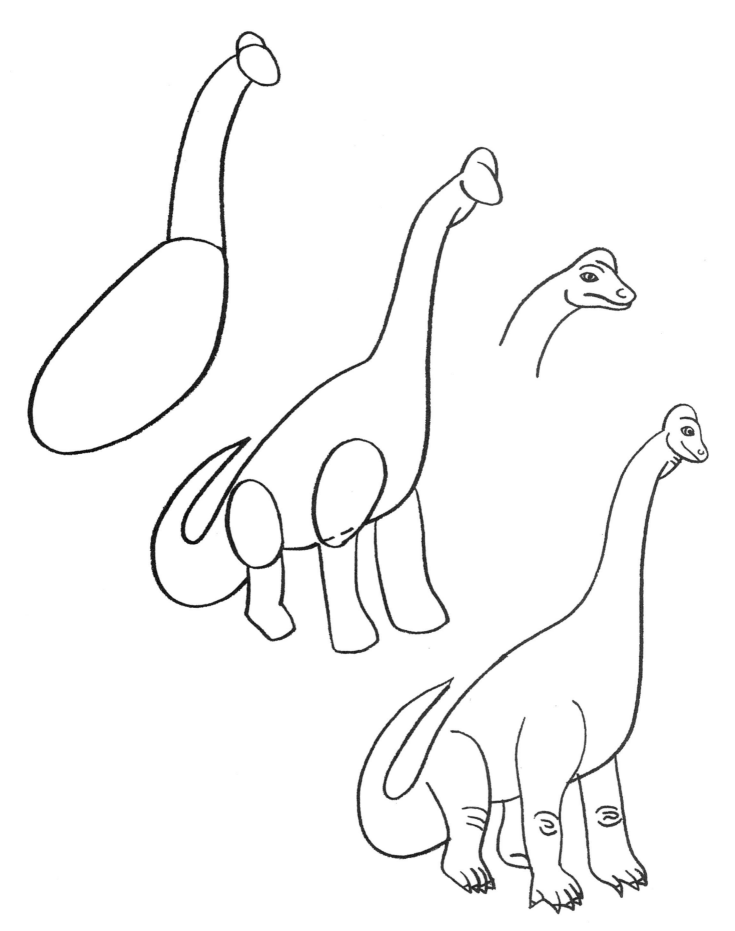

12   Brachiosaurus

Practice Page

14   Brontotherium

Practice Page

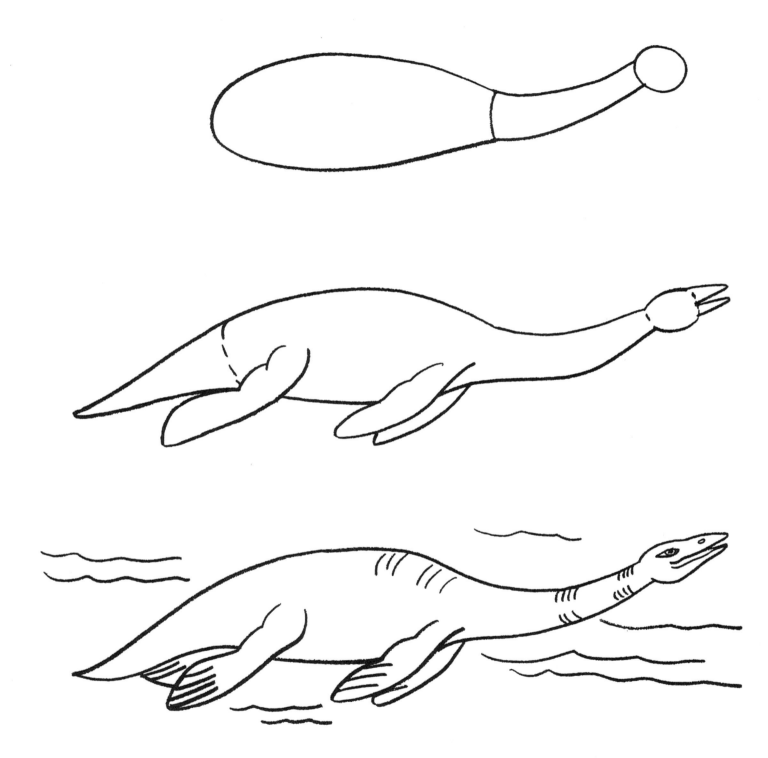

24   Heterodontosaurus

Practice Page

Practice Page

Practice Page

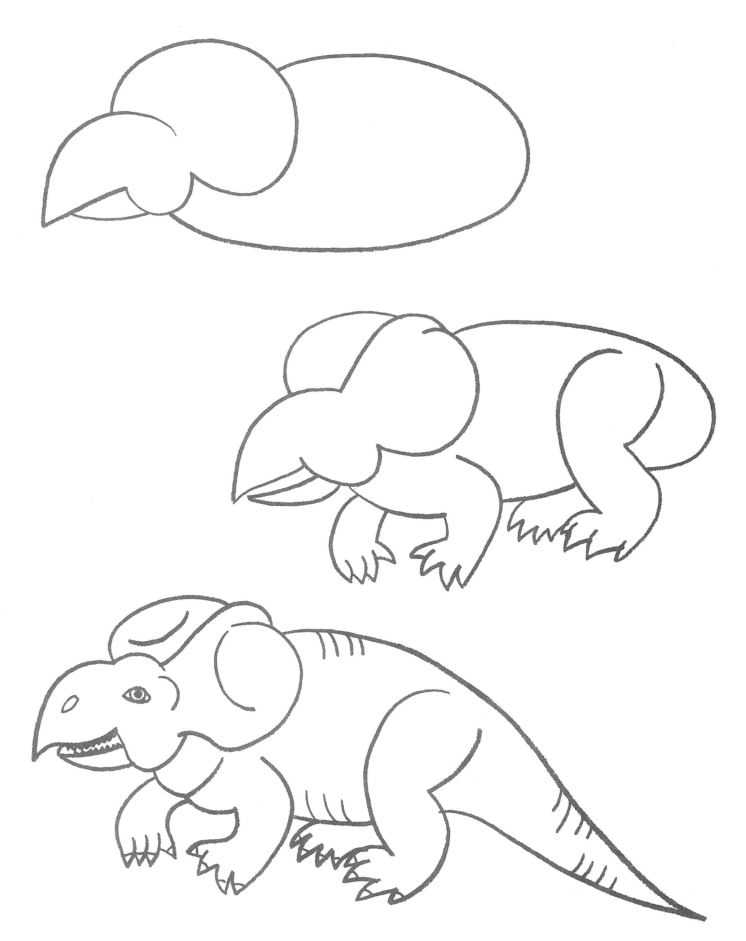

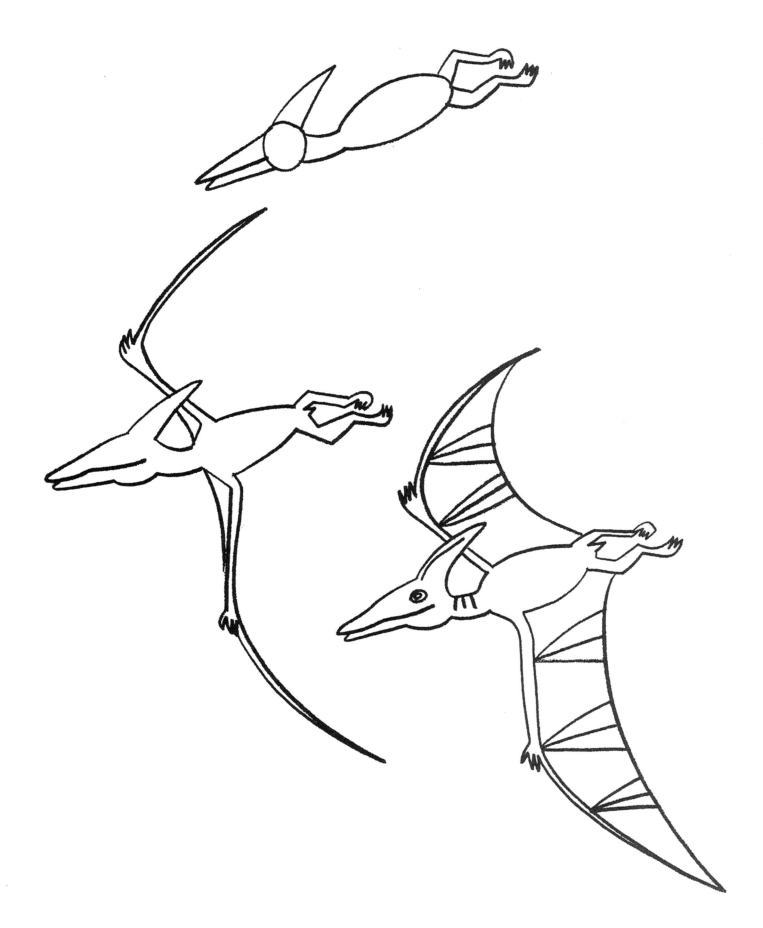

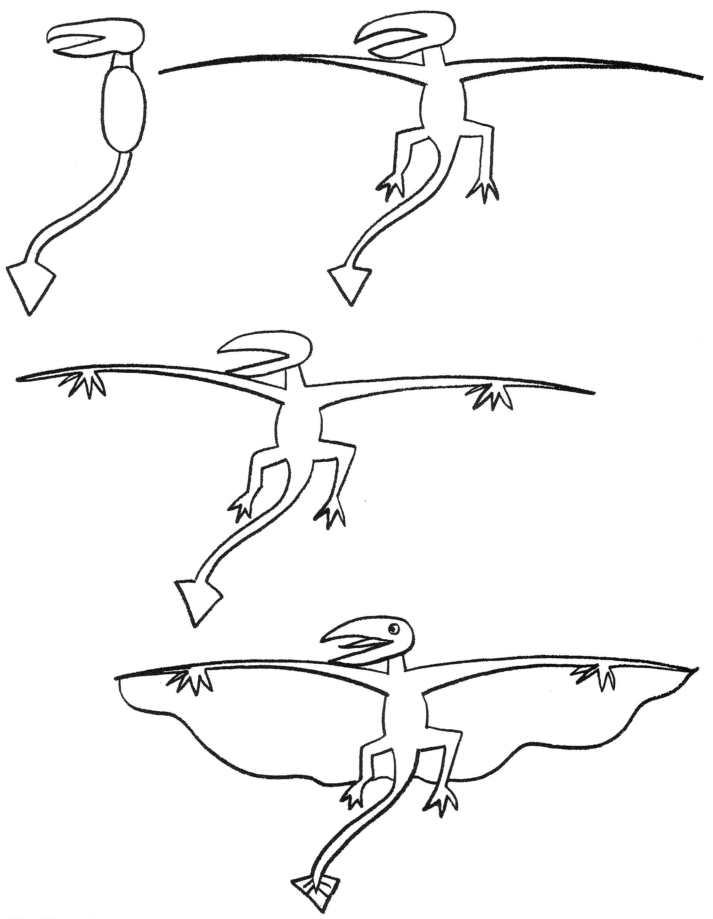

42   Rhamphorhynchus

44   Scutellosaurus

46   Stegosaurus

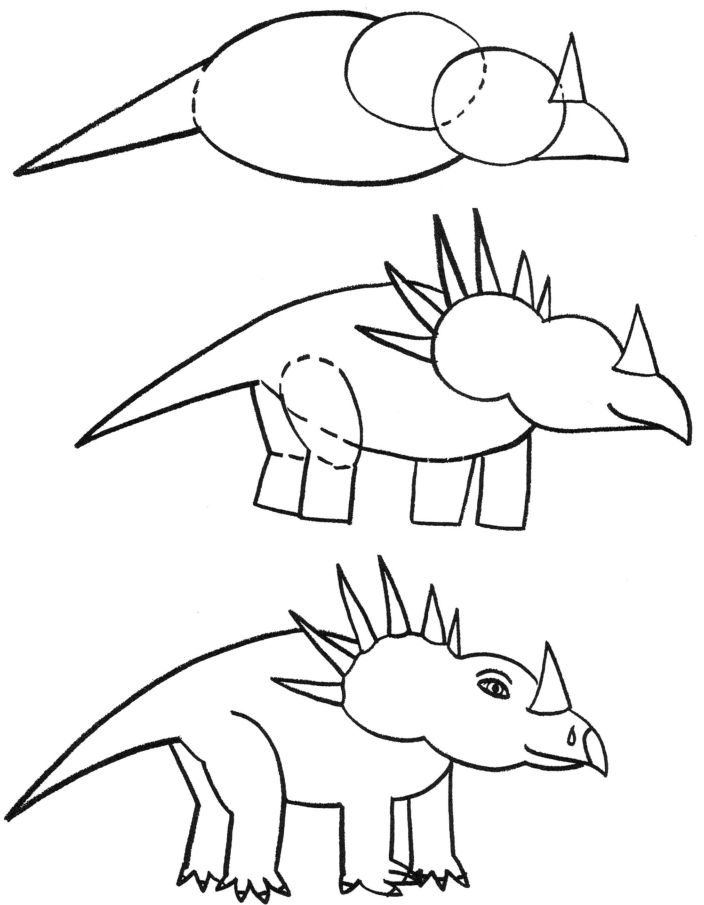

48 Styracosaurus

Practice Page

50   Triceratops

Practice Page

Tylosaurus

54   Tyrannosaurus Rex

Practice Page

Practice Page